Fearless Girl

a guide to facing your fears & achieving your dreams

As pioneers of their best future, we encourage girls to live on a continual quest for *purpose*.

- Fearless Girl Anthem -

Cover and Illustrations: Sereen Gualtieri
Editor: Liberty Joy Fleming

Fearless Girl Co.
www.fearlessgirl.org

- Esther Marie -

For Catie and Sophia— my forever little sisters.
Before Fearless Girl was ever a thing, it was just us learning from each other. You taught me to give my whole heart and when in doubt dance to Taylor Swift like a rockstar.
I am so proud of you both.

For Nick & Chris— thank you for living a fearless life and always challenging me to go beyond my comfort zone to possess God's promises.
No doubt it has shaped who I am today.
I love you both.

For my parents— thank you for never letting me give up on my dreams and teaching me how to dig deep in faith. Your voice of truth has been a firm foundation.
I'm so blessed to be your daughter and I love you both.

For the OG Fearless Girl— Ann Marie, Holly, Therese, Laura, Arisa, Carrie, Lizzy, Alyssa, Lexine, Nicki, Lenox, Sierra and Phoenix. You all have been a part of our journey for the last 3 years and watched Fearless Girl grow from a community into a movement. No doubt, we wouldn't be where we are today without each of you. You each taught me that relationships are the more valuable than opportunity. I love you all and I am so proud of each of you.

- Ebie Hepworth -

Zackery Ikaika- You propel me into my dreams and champion every step of the journey. Thank you for leading our family into a wild and fearless life of faith. I'll never stop loving you.

Granny Sharon + Grandma Rosemary- This book is for you. I come from a lineage of fearless women who paved the way. I love being your granddaughter.

Andra Harris- You have taught me that to be fearless you must be patient, kind, and honest. You'll never know the impact you have had on my life. I love you!

Lisa Bevere- Your life has redefined fearlessness for generations to come. This book is a product of what you have faithfully poured into me. I'll forever be grateful for your voice in my life.

CONTENTS

FORWARD
by Ann Marie

Becoming fearless is not an overnight process; it takes time and a willing heart. My own fearless journey has been a long and arduous one. Although I've gone through some painful hardships, my life began in a happy catholic family with loving parents.

When I think back on my childhood I can remember it like it was yesterday. It was like an old black-and-white projector film, joyous times rolling down hills in barrels with my dad and hours of basketball in the driveway with my brother. I was so carefree and truly fearless.

When I became a teenager, insecurities started to emerge as my self-esteem plummeted. Adults who I thought would be there for me as an emotional support weren't there, especially my father. As disappointment after disappointment continued to hurt me, I started to look for ways to compensate for my lack of confidence. I turned to the easiest substitute-drinking alcohol. At the age of twelve I got blackout drunk for the first time. I felt empty and resentful of anyone I had trusted and drinking was the only thing that gave me a sense of control.

I wanted to stand out and be noticed by those adults who were missing in my life. I was shy, but I felt the urge to rebel to get the attention I craved. Because of my quiet nature, I chose to rebel the best way I knew how- with my appearance. I was enthralled with strong female figures like Joan of Arc, so at the age of sixteen I shaved my entire head and got my first tattoo. At that same time, I started dating a guy who was a skater and six years older than me. He soon became my whole world.

Since I couldn't get the loving connection I needed from my father, I turned to my boyfriend for validation. Every waking moment became about seeing my boyfriend and as a result, I lost all of my girl friends. Our relationship lasted for seven years and my life became a whirlwind of drinking, smoking pot, and experimenting with hallucinogens. I was all about shock value. I became promiscuous and experimented sexually. I couldn't be faithful in my relationships, mainly because I was always getting drunk. I was a mess and tried to hide it from the people who loved me most. It wasn't long before the relationships in my family felt distant as I pushed everyone away to protect my personal sense of independence.

I knew I was living a life that my Catholic mother wouldn't approve of, and I lived with constant guilt because of it. She didn't even have to say a word for me to feel judged and the guilt was tearing me apart. Instead of that guilt making me want to repent or change my ways, the judgement I felt made me want to rebel harder. The idea of religion and God made me feel uncomfortable. I felt like anyone who even uttered the word "Jesus" to me was in a cult and trying to convert me.

I was teetering on the edge of being a normal, working member of society while still dropping acid on the weekends. I struggled with intense anxiety attacks, constantly feeling like the walls were closing in on me. One day at work, I had an anxiety attack that was so bad I couldn't breathe or speak and felt completely paralyzed. All I could do was run outside to my car and call home. My dad picked up and as I sobbed on the phone, he tried to calm me down. I remember in between sobs saying to to him, "Dad, I feel so out of control. If I had a gun in my hand right now I'd shoot myself in the head." I was desperate for freedom and relief, even desperate enough to take my own life. I was having a mental breakdown and didn't leave my house for a week after.

Still, I was far from rock bottom. I continued to dive deep into the bottomless pit of searching for fulfillment in alcohol and began to drink even more heavily. I was out of control! I can recall one occasion where I came into work so completely drunk that I couldn't even keep a straight face. Another time, at my coworker's bachelorette party, I drank so much that a police officer followed our limousine from the bar we had left to our friend's house. When the officer stopped us, he saw how drunk I was and demanded that my friends take me to the ER immediately.

That night at the ER as I got my stomach pumped in an unfamiliar city, with no way home and friends who had left me, you would think that I would have had a wake up call. But I was too afraid of leaving behind a lifestyle I knew all too well...a lifestyle that I thought defined who I was.

In an attempt to find a tangible sense of freedom, I took up surfing. I will never forget how it felt the first time I paddled out beyond the shorebreak and into the large, building waves. Everything was completely quiet and a sense of absolute peace and joy filled my body unlike anything I had ever felt before. When I caught my first wave, it was so freeing, I felt connected to God, something I had never experienced or even knew I longed for. From then on, surfing became my saving grace. It was the only thing that brought me peace and gave me hope. Although I was still struggling with anxiety, a momentous shift started to take place in my life as I pursued this newfound passion.

A few years into my surfing adventure, I came across a post on Facebook by Esther, founder of Fearless Girl. I discovered she was promoting a surf contest to raise awareness about human trafficking, a huge problem that was affecting girls around the world, even right in my own community. I was shocked at this realization and decided to connect with Esther. She invited me to a Fearless Girl meeting at her house to discuss the contest. Although I was nervous about attending, I took the plunge and went to the meeting. When I made my way up the steps to the front door, I didn't know what to expect. I had a brief thought that I could still turn around and go home. But something inside pushed me to keep going. When I knocked on the door, Esther greeted me with a warm embrace, welcoming me into her home. As I sat in the meeting listening to Esther share about her passion to help girls rescued from human trafficking and use surfing as a platform to raise awareness, I was amazed at the opportunity to make a difference while using my passion to surf.

Esther was unlike anyone I had ever met before. Her love for God was so unthreatening and unassuming; it seemed like such a natural extension of who she was. It was the first time I didn't feel uncomfortable with the subject of Jesus and I felt accepted. She shared openly about her faith in a tangible way, and it was the first time I truly saw God's pure light shining through someone. Her joyful personality and pure love for God had a huge impact on me.

That day, I decided to join the Fearless Girl mission and participate in the surf contest. I didn't realize it at the time, but that was the beginning of my journey to true freedom. Through the community of Fearless Girl I began to make significant relationships with other girls who were using their passion of surfing to help others in need. These girls were so encouraging and uplifting and it quickly became a sisterhood for me, something I never had growing up. A change started to take shape in my life as the walls I had built up to keep people out began to come down.

I remember one early morning while surfing, Esther asked me about my faith. In between catching waves, we had a conversation that sparked an interest in me. I had closed the door to religion years ago and decided I didn't want to have anything to do with God. But something about the way Esther talked about her relationship with God made me want to know more. I started to see how God was working around me in other people's lives and I had a desire to have that same relationship with Jesus.

The next week Esther invited me to a conference at her church. It had been ages since I had stepped foot in a church and despite having an anxiety attack just before the conference, I mustered up enough courage to show up. I'll never forget that moment as the worship music played and people began to lift their hands in surrender, tears streamed down my face. The tangible love of God was so real. I didn't feel judged or guilty like I had felt in the past. I felt accepted and for the first time, like I belonged. That night I said yes to Jesus and asked Him to be the savior of my life. I may not have understood it all at the time, but all I know is that the freedom I felt in that moment was greater than any wave I could have ever surfed!

I was elated to have experienced for myself what I had only assumed was exaggerated stories from my Christian friends growing up. Even though I was excited about this new experience, my journey was far from over.

At the time I had been taking anti-depressants by the suggestion of my doctor. About a week after the conference that changed my life, I attended a Halloween party with a few friends. The party was packed with people. There was a half pipe skate ramp in the backyard and rows of storage bins filled with mystery punch labeled according to alcohol strength. It was wild and crazy, but nothing uncommon from what I was used to. It didn't take long for me to jump right in and blend into the scene. At one point someone started switching the labels on the punch. I had no idea what or how much I was drinking and everything became a blur.

I arrived home late that night completely drunk. Still to this day, I have no recollection of what was going through my brain, but in a moment of poor judgement, I finally came face to face with rock bottom as I overdosed on a combination of antidepressants and more hard liquor. A few hours later my boyfriend woke up to me having a seizure and he called 911.

I was in a coma for 24 hours while my family and boyfriend prayed for a miracle. When I came out of the coma at the hospital, it was the most surreal experience of my life. I could hear faraway voices as the doctors started to revive me. It felt like I was in the bottom of a dark well and as I looked up, I could see a light guiding me out. In that moment, I felt like I was being reborn and instantly knew I was being given a second chance by God.

A few days later, Esther came to visit me while I was still in the hospital. I told her that experience served as a huge wake up call and made me look at life differently. I was so aware that God was real and that I was alive for a reason.

I have now been sober for almost a year and am more confident and fearless than I have ever been in my life. I am proud to call myself a Christian and I count my blessings everyday. I have a supportive and loving family, wonderful friends, and a loving boyfriend. Most importantly, I have a relationship with Jesus Christ. He is with me through it all and His love guides me to live my best life.

I can humbly say that I have become fearless because of the confidence God has given me. When I look at myself now, I am astounded by how truly blessed I am. My identity is no longer in a relationship with a guy, how hard I party, or in trying to measure up to what other people think of me.

Sharing my story has been a daunting and truly vulnerable experience. The feelings associated with looking back on where you came from can be difficult, and revealing yourself to others can be scary. But I share it boldly, believing that my story will help another girl find the courage to pursue true freedom. I pray my journey inspires you to never give up, to break out of your comfort zone, to be liberated from the fear that holds you back from pursuing your best life, and finally, to be vulnerable with your story. I have learned that fear holds you back from doing what you know is right, from expressing yourself in your most genuine way, and from enjoying each day with complete satisfaction. That's not the kind of life anyone should live.

Just the simple fact that you are reading this book is a sign that you're searching for more. It's your first step toward true freedom. I'm so proud of you already, and know that you too can live free from fear.

Keep being courageous, girl! You got this!

xoxo,

Ann Marie

INTRODUCTION
by Esther Marie

Snow White sat alone in her parked 1974 Volkswagen Beetle. It was June of 2009, a sweltering hot summer day in southern Florida. Temperatures blazed into the mid 90s- typical Miami weather. Sweat beads dripped down her back as she adjusted her wig and swung her feet out the car window. Yes, Snow White was a fraud. In fact, she was 18 year old me, Esther Marie Gualtieri. At the time I was working as a party Disney princess and had arrived at a 5 year old's birthday party 30 minutes too early to walk in. Mind you, I didn't look like Snow White in the least bit. My wig was a frizzball from the humidity and makeup was melting off my face, making me look more like the Grim Reaper than a Disney princess! Still somehow, I managed to get paid ten dollars an hour.

As I waited in my car for the party to begin I popped in a CD message from one of my new favorite speakers, Lisa Bevere. A few months prior I had a rude awakening to the startling reality that slavery still happens in our world, and I had responded to an inner calling to bring freedom to those enslaved. It was through Lisa's organization that I made this discovery and immediately signed up to volunteer. It was an exciting season as I was discovering my purpose and learning how to respond to the needs in the world.

I remember that moment in my car like it was yesterday. Lisa's message was inspiring and brought me to tears as she prayed for everyone listening. Something powerful shifted beyond what I could explain. I felt free and empowered to fulfill my dreams, and I was never the same.

It's been eight years and during a recent interview with a friend for her school project, I recalled that Snow White moment that had changed my life. I had completely forgotten about that story and recalling it sparked my curiosity to dig up Lisa's message. I listened intently as if it were the first time. In an instant, it seemed as if time had stopped when I heard her say, "A gift lies dormant because of intimidation. But when you face what you fear, you become fearless." My jaw dropped in pure shock. Fearless Girl Company is now three years old and our motto from the very beginning has been: "Face your Fears, Achieve your Dreams." I had no clue back then how much of an impact those words would have on my life. But eight years later, the words spoken over me that day have met me in my future. A seed was planted in my heart that would take years of watering before I could ever see the results.

Fearless Girl was not even a thought until three years ago, but unbeknownst to me all this time I have been walking the fearless journey preparing for this very moment. Living this message out for myself has transformed my life and set me free in every way. It's been a process, not an overnight success. And as I have been traversing through facing my own fears, I have been waiting for you. Yes, you, dear girl, are my dream come true. Your hands grip the binding of a book that only existed in my imagination years ago. I dreamed of you holding it, as you'd embark on your own fearless journey.

My fearless journey has been marked with challenges and setbacks, doubts and uncertainty. Even less than one year ago I didn't know if Fearless Girl Co. would continue to exist. But in the midst of fighting my own battles and practicing what I preach, I was fighting for you and baby girl let me tell you, you are so worth fighting for. I pray that this message equips you to fight your own battles, not to run and hide from fear, but to face it head on with a courageous heart. I pray you discover your purpose, find the freedom to dream again, and say yes to the adventures that await.

Welcome to your fearless journey.

INTRODUCTION
By Ebie Hepworth

I was a sophomore in college when I found myself at one of the most discouraging seasons of my life. I got in my 1999 Toyota Rav4 and started aimlessly driving, hoping to escape my reality. I remember speeding away dramatically because for some reason the sound of my tires spinning out made me feel that much more justified. Blasting Taylor Swift, I pulled off to the side of the road. In my passenger seat sat an invitation to a Christian women's conference where a woman I had never heard of named Lisa Bevere would be speaking. Earlier that day I smiled faintly as I took the invitation out of courtesy from a fellow student athlete. I grew up in the Christian scene and had been to a million of these meetings and decided it wasn't my type of thing. However, as "Dear John" played in the background and I sat alone on the side of the road, I looked at the invitation and realized it was going to be starting in thirty minutes and was right down the road. With tears in my eyes I thought, "Why not?"

I walked into the conference and sat down in the very last row right next to the aisle so that when I got bored I could leave. My exit strategy was planned, and the second a stranger would ask to pray for me, I was going to bounce. But then something happened. The music started to play, my foot began to tap the floor, and my eyes couldn't help but begin to fill with tears. A peace began to wash over my mind, and the broken heart that I walked in with felt like it was being exchanged with something much lighter.

Lisa began speaking and shared a message that was customized to where I was at in that exact moment of life. During the entire message, my face was in my hands, overwhelmed at what I was experiencing. She began sharing about the injustices of human trafficking and invited us to join her in the fight. I had read articles and had seen posts on Facebook, but I assumed that since I wasn't living the right way, my chance at making a positive impact in something like this was absurd. However, something in my heart shifted that night and I wanted to respond not only to have a personal relationship with Jesus, but also to accept the invitation to begin living my life with purpose. I walked out of that conference with a heart transplant and decided to jump into the greatest "yes" of my life. I instantly fell in love with the Holy Spirit and wanted to be a woman who chased after God's heart.

In January of 2014 I became the first U.S. employee of a ministry called Wipe Every Tear, an organization that focuses on bringing hope and healing to precious women that have been rescued from the sex trade in the Philippines. After being with these amazing women, holding their hands, and listening to their dreams, the atrocity of human trafficking suddenly shifted in my mind from being a world problem, to being a family injustice.

Over the years through Wipe Every Tear, through social media, and over coffee dates I have had a front row seat to redemption. I've met fearless girls that have encouraged me to press the limits of my faith and dreams and I've been able to watch first hand hundreds of girls chase after their dreams and realize that BIG dreams are not the goal, but that GOD dreams are the goal.

I had watched Esther unravel Fearless Girl from afar and admired seeing a girl grab a hold of a dream and just go for it. So when our paths finally crossed on a more personal level and Esther opened the door for me to join the ride of sprinting after our purposes together, I remember thinking, "This is the kind of girl I want in my corner. " And that is what Fearless Girl is about. It's not a private club, it's not by invitation only... it's a community of women that are in your corner, opening the door for each other saying, "Come on, we've got stuff to do."

To all my girls who are already responding with the eye roll and shrugged shoulders because I talked about Jesus and sound optimistic, I want to let you know that I've been there. I know what it's like to lose hope. I know what it's like to dismiss faith. But I also know what it's like to experience the freedom and fearlessness that only true love can offer. I hope that through this book, you can begin to experience that as well. My hope is that we all come together from radical backgrounds as if we were in the living room of Heaven, rooting each other on and taking showers in "hallelujahs", asking for more of the real flippin' thing- no counterfeit and no self manufactured idea of what fearlessness is- just stepping into the most organic and authentic version of ourselves that we've ever known. Consider this your open invitation to say "why not" to joining us as we chase after some crazy and radical dreams. I pray this book isn't just another nice thing to read, but that it invites you into a fearless and wild life.

HOW FEARLESS GIRL BEGAN

Have I not commanded you? Be strong and courageous. Do not be afraid; do not be discouraged, for the LORD your God will be with you wherever you go."

-Joshua 1:9-
(NIV)

In 2012 I (Esther) wrote a book for little girls called Twirling Skirts of Magic to encourage them in being themselves and changing the world. In a rough draft of my book, I wrote a line that talked about my main character being a "fearless girl". It didn't make the final edit, but the words "fearless girl" resonated within my soul and a few months after I published my book I launched a blog and called it Fearless Girl. I would write about facing fears and achieving dreams. During this time in my life I had fallen in love with surfing and going on adventures. The only problem was I knew very few girls who surfed and enjoyed adventuring as much as I did. These kinds of activities were male dominant and any time you did come across another girl surfer in the water, it always felt like a competition.

I continued surfing and going on adventures alone, until one day when I met a girl on the beach, Holly, who also surfed alone. We immediately hit it off and became inseparable surf sisters. Through my friendship with Holly I realized the massive need for a network of girls who could surf together, go on adventures, and have genuine community. Girls were feeling isolated and like they had to compete in order to earn respect. I saw this as an opportunity to take the message written in my blog and use it as a way to unite and empower girls in my community. I started a website and Instagram account and began to reach out to girls, encouraging them to face their fears and achieve their dreams. Our network began to grow, meeting weekly for all kinds of adventures and before we knew it, we were planning our first surf contest together as a fundraiser to raise awareness about slavery. During our event we raised over $800 for two organizations and used our passion for adventure for the purpose of changing the world.

For the last three years, Fearless Girl has been operating as a community organization, reaching girls who are isolated and searching for significance. Using the lifestyle of surf and adventure as a tool to connect and share an inspiring message, we have grown into a movement that transcends age or culture. Through the process of developing relationships, engaging in purposeful conversations, and gathering together around one mission, girls have been transformed by this message. In three years we have been able to make a measurable difference in our community, hosting girl-empowering events, inspirational surf clinics for women rescued from sex trafficking, serving as camp counselors, speaking at local school assemblies, and more! Girls who were once struggling to find their identity have found themselves in discovering their purpose.

Today, Fearless Girl is an incorporated lifestyle brand on a mission to guide girls through life's challenges. We are passionate about helping girls face their fears and achieve their dreams. Through our book and online course, girls can discover how to become fearless and live a purpose filled life. The adventure of a lifetime waits! Are you ready?

BECOMING FEARLESS

There is nothing more attractive than a girl who is fearless! There is also nothing more liberating than living free from fear. But the process to becoming fearless is not an easy road. It is a treacherous path leading through battles, hurdles, and the darkest valleys. Although the journey is hard, the reward of freedom is worth it.

Fear is like a disease, covered up by symptoms of issues that arise in our lives. Many of the symptoms that we deal with distract us from dealing with the main issue, which is fear itself. You may struggle with insecurity, intimidation, disappointment, or discouragement, to name a few. But all of these issues are symptoms of the root cause of fear.

Many people will tell you that positive thinking and positive living is the best way to alleviate stress and anxiety. But what yoga and incense can't do for you is expose the main source of turmoil you are experiencing. Stress and anxiety are rooted in fear. Fear hates being called out. It hates being named. It likes to disguise itself as a surface level issue so you live in a constant state of confusion and eventually give up looking for a cure. Fear loves to control, and unfortunately we live in a world where people use fear to negatively manipulate us.

Living free from fear gives you the freedom to live confidently, understand your identity, and know where you are going. And here's the good news: it doesn't need to take a lifetime. You can learn today how to confront your fear at the root.

Through Fearless Girl we share a message of finding freedom from fear, using the captivating imagery of adventure. But adventure alone does not have the power to heal, restore, or bring freedom. Surfing is exhilarating, adventure is fun, but they both still leave us wanting more. Enough is never enough. We are all searching for fullness. Humanity longs for satisfaction. And when we don't find it in our jobs, relationships, or finances, we go bury our lives in obsessive pleasures to distract us from what we truly desire: purpose.

There is only one antidote to the endless search for more- and that is found in an adventure not limited to waves and mountains. The kind of adventure that leaves you feeling wild, free and is not only enough, but MORE than enough. All of a sudden the endless search for more actually transforms into an experience of a more that doesn't leave you empty, but overflowing. This discovery is essential to life, it's essential to humanity and it's essential to becoming a Fearless Girl.

The adventure I'm talking about is found in having a relationship with Jesus Christ, the One who came to forgive us of our sins, offer us freedom from fear, and fulfill every dream in our heart. Before you put this book back on the shelf because you didn't realize it was going to be "religious"- I ask you to WAIT! Don't judge a book by it's cover...or actually maybe you should because the cover of this book is pretty epic! Keep reading and have an open mind. What are you afraid of? After all, isn't that why you started reading this book? Something about being fearless compelled you and drew you in. Are you struggling with anxiety, insecurity, doubt, depression, OCD, or another kind of fear? If so, that's no way to go through life, full of limits and "I cant's".

We have come up with a formula to equip you in becoming fearless. It's not a secret magic sauce (unfortunately, otherwise we'd smother that goodness all over our tacos). Instead, this formula serves as a guide- a map, like you would get upon entering your favorite national park. I have a map of Yosemite National Park sitting in my glove compartment of my car right now. But just because I have that map doesn't mean I'm an expert at navigating Yosemite. I have to first study the map, explore each path, discover the best routes, and experience the journey the map lays out for me.

In the same way, we have laid out a strategy in this book that will guide you to confront your fears and achieve your dreams. But until you take the first step and then embark on the journey by applying what you learn to your daily life, you will never experience the freedom that awaits you on the other side of your fear.

Facing your fears and achieving your dreams is a lot like climbing a mountain. But mountains are not conquered easily. It's a process taken one step at a time as you carefully navigate rough terrain, obstacles, weather changes, and unforeseen challenges. Conquering the mountains of your fears and achieving your dreams takes commitment to staying the course.

A few years ago, my friend Sierra and I decided to take a spontaneous trip up to Yosemite Valley to fulfill our dream of hiking Half Dome. It was a 16 mile hike that took us 11 hours as we reached 8,839ft elevation. When we reached the sub dome we were only about thirty minutes from reaching the top, but after hours of climbing, this point in our journey proved to be the most difficult. As we stopped to take a short break, I turned the corner to find a woman lying down in between two rocks with her shoes off and her hands over her face. I immediately went over to make sure she was okay. Startled by my friend and I, she sat up and explained to us what had happened. She was a middle-aged woman named Alexis and she had a panic attack while hiking with her husband. She was so afraid that something bad would happen to them and couldn't get passed her fear so she gave up and told her husband to go on without her. I sat down next to Alexis and began to encourage her. She was so close to reaching the top...I couldn't let her give up that easily! As my friend and I spoke to her, light began to enter her eyes and courage entered her heart. We invited her to hike with us and committed to patiently walk the rest of the journey with her. Alexis was so encouraged, she put her shoes back on and started hiking with us. When we approached the dome we still had 100 ft of steep climbing left with cables to hold onto. This, by far, was the most dangerous part of the hike. I went ahead and positioned Alexis in the middle between me and Sierra and told her not to be afraid because we were with her. The climb was steep and scary. Every few steps I'd turn back and check on Alexis. "How are you feeling? Just take it one step at a time. There's no rush. You're doing great." As we reached the top of Half Dome, I got to record Alexis surprising her husband as she not only fulfilled her dream, but conquered her fear!

Alexis was totally fearless as she stepped out to face her fear and achieve her dream. There is a verse in the bible that says, "This is my command--be strong and courageous! Do not be afraid or discouraged. For the Lord your God is with you wherever you go." (Joshua 1:9, NIV). There's a difference between feeling afraid and being afraid. Being afraid is allowing the feeling of fear to stop you from achieving your dream, letting fear deplete you of strength and rob you of your purpose. When the feeling of fear comes you have a choice to either give up and hide away in your fears, or let God's presence give you strength to keep going.

Watching Alexis overcome her fear and achieve her dream gave my moment on Half Dome priceless value! It gave it purpose beyond myself. Are you, like Alexis, allowing fear to rob you of your dream? Maybe it's fear of what other people think about you. Fear of failing. Fear of being rejected. Fear of missing out. Fear of commitment. We want you to know that God has gone before you, just like I went before Alexis and journeyed with her. He is saying, "baby, I'm with you. You can do this. Don't be afraid!"

Just like Alexis was able to conquer her mountain of fear and achieve her dream, we want to equip you with the guide to conquer your mountain! Using the mountain theme as an illustration, we have mapped out a course to lead you through confronting your fears and achieving your dreams:

Base Camp 1: Recognize your insecurities. Insecurity is the first sign that fear is eating away at your dream. Insecurity causes you to feel inadequate and incapable of greatness and it overcompensates to impress others. Pride is at the root of insecurity, and fear is at the root of pride. Admitting your insecurity and locating the areas of your weakness is step one.

Base Camp 2: Face your fear. Our initial reaction when we encounter fear is to run from it. But facing our fear is the first step to overcoming it. Position yourself to engage with your fear head on. Do the daring thing by making the call, submitting the application, having the conversation, signing up for the contest, or whatever it might be. TAKE ACTION to face that fear.

Base Camp 3: Identify the lie. Many fears are built out of the lies we have believed about ourselves. We build false realities out of these lies and anticipate negative outcomes. Lies deceive you to believe that you will never find freedom from your past or present torment. These lies try to convince you to give up and settle for a "good enough" life. You can learn to recognize these lies by discerning the voice that condemns you. Lies always tear you down, but you can choose to reject them and replace them with truth.

Base Camp 4: Discover the truth. There is a voice of truth that is speaking to you always. It is our responsibility to tune our ear to recognize this voice and follow it. Eventually the lies that we have believed will fade away and the truth will outlive any deceptions. The voice of truth always speaks life and encouragement. It inspires positive imaginations and unveils traps that could cause you to lose traction as you realize your dreams. Experiencing a relationship with Jesus is the breaking point to finding truth. He is the truest truth that will set you free from every deception.

Peak of Mountain 5: Experience freedom. Freedom is found in total surrender as you reach the top of your mountain. You are free from the struggle, you have faithfully stayed the course and overcame your fears. You can rest, breath, and take in the sights with your mountain now under your feet. You don't have to fight anymore. You don't have to strive. You have won the battle. You are free to dream again. But your mountain top experience is not just for you. It is FOR freedom that you have been set free. And with your mountain of fear now beneath you, it is the power is in your hand to lend freedom to those still living in fear. Your journey is not yet over.

Completion of Journey 6: Achieve your dream. Now that you have overcome your fear and conquered your mountain, it is time for you to dig deep into your purpose and achieve your dreams. You must journey onward and move into new territory of possessing the promises of God. Your purpose comes alive in new beginnings as you do the hard work of diligence to bring your dream to pass. Now is not the time to settle or give up. It's time to enter into your destiny and achieve your dreams with your fears now behind you.

These six steps are designed as a guide to help you navigate your personal journey of facing your fears and achieving your dreams. I dare you to stick with this book and apply these principles to your life and see the results of becoming fearless in all you pursue. Maybe you thought you could never do a particular thing. This book will empower you to have faith in yourself. Maybe you thought you could never be a Christian or have a relationship with Jesus. This book will help you see past the stigmas placed on Christianity and teach you how to have faith in God. His love is written for you on every mountain. He faithfully pursues your heart and attention with every wave. His love knows no bounds. Everything in creation is designed to captivate your heart and invite you into the adventure of faith. You might be surprised at how exhilarating and freeing it actually is to allow yourself to have faith. This book will empower you to overcome every big or little fear you may have and give you practical guidance to achieving the dreams within your heart.

May you courageously pioneer through unknown terrain, overcome the obstacles of doubt, and ever thirst for a continual quest to lay hold of your purpose. May you become fearless as your mountains find their place in the rear view mirror of your life. May your dreams come alive as you dance, wild and free as you flourish in all that you have been created to be.

May you become a Fearless Girl.

30 DAILY DOSES OF COURAGE

Fear of Taking Risks
(Esther)

Surfing is an incredible sport that has taught me how to be a risk taker. There can be a risk of getting injured or even dying while surfing. The stakes are always high and there is no guarantee that you won't get bruised, cut, or held under by a wave. There's also a slight chance of encountering a visit from a great white shark! You might be wondering why I still continue to surf when the risks are so high. Beyond the exhilarating experience of catching waves, surfing gives me an opportunity to taste a fearless moment.

As a wave rolls in, it's as if the ocean is saying to me, "I dare you to be fearless." In that moment I have two options: either allow fear to paralyze me or take the risk! The first option keeps me safe inside the boundaries of my comfort zone. The second pushes me outside of my comfort zone and gives me the opportunity to build my confidence. As I make the decision, I'm always reminded of my favorite verse, "Fearless now, I trust in God," (Psalm 56:11 MSG). I find a freedom to be brave as I trust in God and decide to be fearless.

Face your fear, achieve your dream

Taking risks is the ultimate test of confidence. Do you believe in yourself enough to give up the comfort of where you are in order to attain the reward on the other side of your risk? Are you facing decisions that feel risky and you're tempted to stay in your comfort zone? Take some time away from stressing over your situation. Do things outside your comfort zone like hiking to a high elevation, singing in front of a crowd, dancing in public, or spending time serving others in need. God will use every step of faith you take to guide you through the risk you take. Any step taken in faith is a step in the right direction. The confidence we are looking for will only come when we step out to DO it. So trust in God as he makes you fearless to achieve your dreams!

Fearless Girl

Use this outline as a guide to help you overcome your fear.

Recognize Your Insecurities: _____

_____

Face Your Fear: _____

_____

Identify The Lie: _____

_____

Discover The Truth: _____

_____

Find Freedom: _____

_____

Achieve Your Dream: _____

_____

Fear of Rejection
(Ebie)

I may be biased, but me and my husband's love story is one of my all-time favorite stories. Without going into crazy detail, I was friend-zoned for about two years before we started dating (insert the long sighhhh). I started majorly crushing on him about 5 months after we met and didn't want to tell a soul. Early on, Zac and I were talking and he randomly said, "I honestly don't know if I'll ever get married." I remember wishing I could melt into the seat and disappear. He had no idea at the time how I felt about him, but hearing him say those words made me feel like I had just face planted into the concrete. It was more what he DIDN'T say that froze me with feelings of inadequacy and rejection. I wanted him to express his love, but he didn't give me any validation. The fear of rejection occurs when we place our value and validation in how someone else sees us.

What man fails to acknowledge, God sees. He shouts, "I see you and I'm so proud of you." When we accept that his seal of approval is enough, we'll watch the fear of rejection wash away. Hear this, my friend, the world rejected God so that you could be approved by heaven. Do not dilute his approval and admiration of you!

Face your fear, achieve your dream
Do you know what apple trees are good for? Growing apples. Do you know what avocado trees are not good for? Growing apples. Are you tracking with me? Avocado trees stink at being apple trees. What I am getting at here is that God desires for you to be great for YOUR designed purpose. When we are busy living in fear of rejection, we are not living out our intended purpose! Overcoming this fear is found in truly understanding where your value comes from and running fearlessly toward what God has called us to do. In moments when we can feel rejection trying to wiggle its unwanted self into our hearts, what if we turned our attention to the value that God has granted us? what if we recognized that it's the enemy's favorite tactic to steal and kill our worth and that the rejection we are feeling isn't real because we know our worth in the Kingdom. Get a hold of this truth and watch the rest of your life radically change.

Fearless Girl

Use this outline as a guide to help you overcome your fear.

Recognize Your Insecurities: _____

_____

Face Your Fear: _____

_____

Identify The Lie: _____

_____

Discover The Truth: _____

_____

Find Freedom: _____

_____

Achieve Your Dream: _____

Fear of Missing Out
(Esther)

Scrolling through my Instagram feed can sometimes send me into a downward spiral of serious FOMO (fear of missing out). As I see my friends posting epic pictures of their adventures snowboarding, surfing, and traveling the world (#PNW #TheGreatOutdoors #HikeSomething #AdventureIsLife), immediately my life feels insignificant and I begin to envy their adventures. If only I didn't have specific time commitments, then I wouldn't have to miss out so much!

Social media can be a powerful tool used for positive intentions or a powerful weapon used for ill intent. The reality is that watching someone's highlight reel isn't an accurate depiction of life. No one is going to Instagram themselves brushing their teeth, putting on deodorant, taking out the trash, or changing their cat's litter box. Instagram is great for sharing experiences, but it can lead us down a road of comparison, wishing our lives were as weird as the Kardashians.

Let's be real though, life is better when you are satisfied and content. The fear of missing out can cause us to lose a sense of significance and creativity in our lives. FOMO not only gives us a crummy feeling, but it robs us of the joy of celebrating others. The Bible says, "So be content with who you are, and don't put on airs. God's strong hand is on you; he'll promote you at the right time," (1Peter 5:6 MSG)

Face your fear, achieve your dream

FOMO creates anxiety out of thin air. But I have good news! You have the power to CHOOSE what you will focus on. Choose to direct your thoughts towards what you have instead of what you wish you had. Change your perspective of Instagram and be watchful of who you follow and what you post. Save some adventures for yourself. When you see a cool adventure posted by your friend, call them and ask them how it went. Don't let FOMO make you an adventure snob. Celebrate your friends and be inspired by their wins!

Fearless Girl

Use this outline as a guide to help you overcome your fear.

Recognize Your Insecurities: _____

_____

Face Your Fear: _____

_____

Identify The Lie: _____

_____

Discover The Truth: _____

_____

Find Freedom: _____

_____

Achieve Your Dream: _____

Fear of Being Vulnerable
(Ebie)

Ugh. Vulnerability- the word alone makes me cringe. Identifying my emotions is not something that comes naturally to me. I used to convince myself that being vulnerable exposed my weaknesses and was girly and unnecessary. I believed the lie that if I ignored my emotions and insecurities, they'd eventually go away. This logic says, "If I turn my back to the ocean, maybe the waves will stop coming in." How ridiculous! Facing this fear is necessary, but guess what is waiting for you on the other side of vulnerability? Freedom. Hear me out girlfriend, being vulnerable takes courage! And you were made to be courageous!

One of the most vulnerable seasons of my life was when I was 20, about to graduate college. I knew that I wanted to devote my life to fighting the injustices of human trafficking, but had no clue what step to take. I got word of this incredible internship in Colorado, but it would require moving, potential loneliness, strenuous hours, and learning a new job. It would require vulnerability. Months later I found myself driving through a snowstorm to Colorado Springs to begin that internship. And do you know what? That season of training, equipping, and learning activated me to where I am now.

I am convinced that when we are vulnerable, whether with our emotions, time, or willingness to try something new, all of Heaven roars with excitement. Had I not been vulnerable with my life and my gifts, I would have robbed myself of one of the greatest seasons of my life! Do you really want that dream, that adventure, and that breakthrough? Because it lies on the other side of vulnerability. It's the secret ingredient to being unstoppable and wild!

Face your fear, achieve your dream

Maybe, like me, the word vulnerability makes you cringe. I have found that before I can ever be vulnerable with myself or others, I need to bring it to God in my quiet time. And can I tell you something? In all the times I have shared something vulnerable with Jesus, he has never responded with, "I don't care, you're ridiculous, Ebie." Each and every time He's responded in love and gentleness. Being vulnerable with the Lord will infuse confidence into your spirit, allowing you to run with purpose and excitement toward freedom!

Fearless Girl

Use this outline as a guide to help you overcome your fear.

Recognize Your Insecurities: _____

_____

Face Your Fear: _____

_____

Identify The Lie: _____

_____

Discover The Truth: _____

_____

Find Freedom: _____

_____

Achieve Your Dream: _____

Fear of the Unknown
(Esther)

During the filming of our online course in Yosemite, we were hiking a trail when we came to a sign that said, "Caution: Rock Fall. Enter at Own Risk." The sun had gone down and it was pitch black. Ebie turned to me and said, "Esther, this is not a good sign." I looked ahead at the path. There was a waterfall that we would have to run through and face any roadblocks ahead. The path was uncertain. But I knew it well. "Ebie, I've hiked this path several times. Trust me!"

As we continued down the path, our flashlights revealed snowy mounds, fallen trees, and massive rocks that blocked our way. We could only see as far as the step in front of us as the flashlights illuminated our path. It was a treacherous way to end our hike and we didn't finish until 10pm that night. In the end, our favorite part of the hike was when we ran through the waterfall. Although, it was cold and scary, once we were safe, we felt invigorated!

When faced with an uncertain situation, we have the option to recoil in fear, or view the unknowns as an invitation to be courageous! God tells us, "I will instruct you and teach you in the way you should go…" (Psalm 32:8 NIV). Just like Ebie had to trust me to guide the group down the path, we need to trust God to instruct us in our daily lives.

Face your fear, achieve your dream

What unknowns are haunting you today? Is it uncertainty about what school you will get into? Or if your test results will come back positive? You may not know what's to come, but everything you don't know will be revealed at just the right time. Approach your situation as an opportunity to grow and let go of always trying to be in control. The wild unknown is meant for the brave, adventurous ones who take the less traveled roads. Practice filtering your thoughts as your mind wanders and find certainty in God as you trust Him to guide you.

Fearless Girl

Use this outline as a guide to help you overcome your fear.

Recognize Your Insecurities: _____

_____

Face Your Fear: _____

_____

Identify The Lie: _____

_____

Discover The Truth: _____

_____

Find Freedom: _____

_____

Achieve Your Dream: _____

Fear of Being Misunderstood
(Ebie)

This is, without a doubt, one of my greatest fears. I've been so wrapped up in wondering if someone misunderstood my heart that I've made myself physically sick. I'd like to think it stems from a delicate and tender heart, but unfortunately it stems from an insecure one that always wants to be liked. For some absurd reason we think that if someone misunderstands us, our integrity is on the line. I've encountered this fear at Wipe Every Tear when I've had to confront a team member about how they could've handled a situation in a better way. Each time I approach these conversations, I've been afraid that the person would take it the wrong way and not understand my heart for correction, to the point where I have almost avoided many of these conversations. "I don't want to make her feel judged or not appreciated," is my go-to excuse, when the reality is that BECAUSE I appreciate her I want to empower and equip her.

If you're like me, you feel things deeply, sometimes making it hard to process those feelings ourselves let alone trying to clearly communicate them. We become so afraid of being perceived wrongly that we retreat from vulnerability. But we have to understand that there is grace for communication in relationships! We need to be willing to both give and receive grace when attempting to share our hearts. Showing this grace and being intentional with our words and soft with our tone will go a long way! We might not always get our point across perfectly, but being fearless is being vulnerable!

Face your fear, achieve your dream

There are three keys to facing this fear. First, recognize the fact that you will never be misunderstood by God. He knows you and He loves you, and he understands what your words could never communicate. Rest in that knowledge. Next, face this fear by understanding the root of feeling misunderstood. I have found that when I feel misunderstood, it was usually because I was rambling in circles in a conversation and honestly not making any sense. I was simply talking to talk. When I realized this, I became more focused on listening instead of responding. This helped me to be more intentional with my responses, relieving the fear of being misunderstood. Lastly, come to peace with the fact that not everyone will understand your heart! That is OK! God will bring the right people into your life at the right time who will understand you perfectly.

Fearless Girl

Use this outline as a guide to help you overcome your fear.

Recognize Your Insecurities: _____

_____

Face Your Fear: _____

_____

Identify The Lie: _____

_____

Discover The Truth: _____

_____

Find Freedom: _____

_____

Achieve Your Dream: _____

Fear of Heartbreak
(Esther)

When we experience heartbreak, whether through a break-up, losing a loved one, or losing something of great value, it can be tempting to build a wall around our heart. C.S Lewis really puts this into perspective:

"To love at all is to be vulnerable. Love anything and your heart will be wrung and possibly broken. If you want to make sure of keeping it intact you must give it to no one, not even an animal. Wrap it carefully round with hobbies and little luxuries; avoid all entanglements. Lock it up safe in the casket or coffin of your selfishness. But in that casket, safe, dark, motionless, airless, it will change. It will not be broken; it will become unbreakable, impenetrable, irredeemable. To love is to be vulnerable." (The Four Loves, p. 169)

I experienced my first relationship heartbreak a few years ago. Our relationship was great for a while, but eventually our vast differences came to the surface and the relationship dissolved. I had never cared about someone that deeply. When the relationship failed, my heart hurt like never before. It became difficult for me to trust again. I built a wall around my heart and didn't want to let anyone in because I was so afraid of experiencing another heartbreak.

A few months after, I attended a conference in Australia where I met some incredible guys who were outstanding examples of men who valued women. One guy in particular made me feel so special. I realized that I had dramatically lowered my belief of what I deserved in a relationship. This guy showed me how a man should value a woman and although we never dated, he helped me tear down the walls I had built around my heart. Through that friendship I experienced the reality of this verse, "The Lord is near to the brokenhearted." (Psalm 34:18 ESV). I knew God wanted the best for me and he gave me an opportunity to catch glimpse of what that could look like.

Face your fear, achieve your dream

Are you afraid of letting someone close or committing to a new relationship? What dream is being withheld because of the fear of heartbreak? Don't allow past heartbreakers to steal your dream and hold you prisoner to your past. Talk to someone about your attachment to that heartbreak and make a decision today that you aren't going to stay broken. Be encouraged, love is on the way and it will be worth the wait.

Fearless Girl

Use this outline as a guide to help you overcome your fear.

Recognize Your Insecurities: _____

_____

Face Your Fear: _____

_____

Identify The Lie: _____

_____

Discover The Truth: _____

_____

Find Freedom: _____

_____

Achieve Your Dream: _____

Fear of Letting People Down
(Ebie)

...AKA the fear of imperfection. Oh boy, I can relate on this one! Because I have two older brothers and played 18 years of soccer, being competitive and always desiring the 1st place trophy is like second nature to me. From a young age this fear took root in my heart and began to manifest as anxiety. I felt suffocated by my to-do lists and was held captive by responsibilities, all because I didn't want to let anyone down. I only experienced peace when I felt like I was succeeding and even then I was still anxious that failure was right around the corner.

I distinctly remember the Lord once telling me, "Elizabeth, the fear of letting people down is the root of your anxiety. Since when did pleasing them become more important than spending time with me?" Being obedient to the adventure God is taking you on must always take precedence to our fears. And let me tell you, once you've tasted the true peace of Jesus, when you've walked with it, when you've been carried by it- you know that there could never be a sufficient substitute for it. Don't get me wrong, doing things with excellence is one thing, but constantly living your life in a state of fear wondering if you're letting someone down will cripple the calling on your life.

Face your fear, achieve your dream
One of my favorite things about worship is the peace that floods my spirit, mind, and body. The beautiful truth is that there is no need for striving in our relationship with Jesus. Where my eyes were once on a to-do list, I now find them just gazing at Jesus. No striving, no pressure, no performing, just soaking in who he has called me to be. It is effortless and our most natural state of being! So what is your favorite way to worship? Maybe it is going on a long run in the mountains. Maybe it is grabbing a cup of coffee and watching the waves roll in. Regardless, find that sweet and intimate place of worship and embrace the truth that you are not letting your heavenly father down when you're unified with Him! This will deposit strength and grace into your spirit, allowing your mind to not be offended when something isn't completed to perfection. This new strength and grace will soon become the navigation system for your spirit, something so natural and sweet that you will always want to cultivate it.

Fearless Girl

Use this outline as a guide to help you overcome your fear.

Recognize Your Insecurities: _____

_____

Face Your Fear: _____

_____

Identify The Lie: _____

_____

Discover The Truth: _____

_____

Find Freedom: _____

_____

Achieve Your Dream: _____

Fear of Not Being Good Enough
(Esther)

It can be hard for us girls to believe we are good enough sometimes. Measuring up seems unattainable when we're surrounded by a world of beauty and talent. When I was a teenager, I teetered on the edge of an eating disorder as I hated my appearance and couldn't see my true worth. Other girls seemed to have it all- tall, luscious hair, and perfect skin. Standing next to them, I felt like a middle school nerd with braces who was unbearably awkward. These girls appeared like the chosen ones who could get any guy they wanted. But the reality wasn't that I was ugly or that these girls were perfect. The root of my insecurity was in the way I saw myself that resulted in my feeling inferior.

We live in a world of comparison where the measure of a person is determined by human standards. When we measure ourselves against others we will always lose. No matter what kind of car you drive, it's never cool enough. No matter how much money you have, someone else always has more. No matter how famous you are, the attention is never enough.

Well, I have good news for you: you will NEVER be good enough. Really though, that is good news! NOTHING in this life will ever be ENOUGH to measure your worth. You were made with eternal value and only your Maker can affirm your worth. The fear of not being good enough comes from a place of envy. We want what someone else has, whether it's their looks, talent, or material things, and then out of inferiority we begin to compare ourselves to them. This mindset will always leave us feeling empty. Matthew 11:28 says, "Come to me, all who labor and are heavy laden, and I will give you rest" (ESV). The fear of never being good enough is an endless cycle. God offers you rest and total confidence that you are perfect just the way you are.

Face your fear, achieve your dream
Do you battle with thoughts of being inferior around people who appear more talented or attractive? Do you work tirelessly and strive to be the best, but never seem to measure up? Perhaps your efforts seem like they are lacking because you have lost sight of your true worth. Earthly measurements could never equate your true value. Only an eternal measurement created by God could accurately define your worth. Make a list of 10 things you like about yourself. Recite this list out-loud in front of the mirror and ask God to help you see yourself the way He sees you.

Fearless Girl

Use this outline as a guide to help you overcome your fear.

Recognize Your Insecurities: _____

_____

Face Your Fear: _____

_____

Identify The Lie: _____

_____

Discover The Truth: _____

_____

Find Freedom: _____

_____

Achieve Your Dream: _____

Fear of Getting Hurt
(Esther)

On a trip to Mexico, I was separated from my friends while surfing. The waves weren't too big that day, so I wasn't worried. All of a sudden, a huge set of waves appeared out of nowhere! I began to paddle as hard as I could, but it was too late. The monster wave came crashing down, taking me down with it! I tumbled underwater for the greatest ocean beating of my life, only to resurface and get pounded again by another giant wave! Thankfully, I fought through and made it out of the ocean that day with just a few bruises and a renewed respect for the ocean.

After that experience, it was harder for me to surf the rest of the trip. Each time I paddled out, my previous wipe out replayed in my mind like a broken record. Afraid that the same thing would happen again, I held back. I couldn't commit. I was afraid of getting hurt again and lost trust in my ability to be a strong surfer.

I wasn't too proud of myself for allowing fear to ruin a great trip and refused to allow that incident to rob me of my passion forever. After that experience, I had to rebuild my confidence while surfing. I overcame my fear of getting hurt by practicing being courageous. I was determined to not allow memories from the past to dictate my future.

There is a healthy fear that helps us to avoid danger, but when the fear of getting hurt hinders you from enjoying your life, it becomes a problem.

Face your fear, achieve your dream

The fear of getting hurt is a result of a lack of trust. Either we don't trust other people, ourselves, or we don't trust God. Sometimes, we make choices that cause us to get hurt. Sometimes other people hurt us and it's not our fault. Although, we are not promised a pain free life, God can be trusted to guide you through painful times. What is causing you to be afraid of getting hurt? Is it issues within family relationships? Have you been betrayed and are afraid of it recurring? Stop bracing yourself for the worst! Stop replaying the past. Realize that the opportunity in front of you is a chance to start over. TRUST God! He will guide you with your best interest in mind and lead you into your dreams.

Fearless Girl

Use this outline as a guide to help you overcome your fear.

Recognize Your Insecurities: _____

_____

Face Your Fear: _____

_____

Identify The Lie: _____

_____

Discover The Truth: _____

_____

Find Freedom: _____

_____

Achieve Your Dream: _____

Fear of Being Discontent
(Ebie)

Remember that childhood song, "First comes love, then comes marriage, then comes a baby in a baby carriage! That's not all, that's not all…" We've been ingraining the concept of "the next thing" into our minds since we were kids on the playground! We are obsessed with MORE. Before I say anything else, understand that there is a vast difference between anticipating and hoping for the future and being so focused on it that you miss out on the here and now.

Some girls fear discontentment in the "normal" everyday life so much that they are always seeking more, busying themselves and not appreciating their current life. They are so obsessed with next that they sacrifice their joy, relationships, work life, and health now. They become blind to the value that is in front of them.

Friend, I don't want you to miss something because you were distracted by the fear of discontentment! Instead of fearing discontentment, we need to simply learn how to be content! Being content is the secret to a rich and fulfilled life. When we fully embrace each season, we find peace and joy and are able to grow. Discontentment clouds our vision, distorts our thinking, and robs us of a sound mind. But a content heart recognizes the value of each season and allows us to get everything we can out of it. It does not mean that we become complacent! Actually, when we are content and embrace the growth that is available in every season, we end up dreaming bigger and having more passion for the future than ever before! But instead of looking to the future because we are lacking something, we start to look to the future to BUILD upon what we have already started!

Face your fear, achieve your dream

We have to combat this fear with an intentional lifestyle of gratitude. We need to be grateful through our thoughts, words, and actions. What if we became so overwhelmed in thankfulness that the fear of discontentment began to just melt away? There is no such thing as being thankful and discontent at the same time, it's impossible! Start to recognize the value of the things that are currently in your life. There will be joy and peace in the future, but it is available right in this moment too! Embracing each season and being grateful for what is around you will lead to a life of fulfillment and joy!

Fearless Girl

Use this outline as a guide to help you overcome your fear.

Recognize Your Insecurities: _____

_____

Face Your Fear: _____

_____

Identify The Lie: _____

_____

Discover The Truth: _____

_____

Find Freedom: _____

_____

Achieve Your Dream: _____

_____

Fear of Change
(Esther)

Summer is my all time favorite season. As I'm writing this, California is transitioning from summer into fall. I'm always sad to see summer go and I protest it as long as possible by wearing shorts and flip flops well into winter. But no matter how long I fight it, the seasons will change.

For some, change is invigorating. For others, change is stressful and feels like the entire world is crumbling. Whichever category you fall into, one thing is certain- change is unavoidable. Life is full of changing seasons. When I was 21, I moved from Miami, Florida to Huntington Beach, California, nearly 3,000 miles away from home! I realized this was a HUGE change and I spent the next five years learning how to navigate adulthood. It was hard, painful, and I went through a period of grieving the life I had left behind.

I can remember standing in line for security after saying a tearful goodbye to my family on the day that I moved. I became so fearful of the change about to take place, and uncertain if I was really doing the right thing. With tears streaming down my face, I handed my ticket to the security agent. As I began to walk away he stopped me and said, "I know right now it's really hard and for a time it's going to hurt, but God wants you to know you're going to be ok. You're going to be so happy." In that moment, it felt as though God reached down from heaven and gave me the biggest hug.

Change hurts and it is difficult, but if we embrace it and move forward, we will grow into our full potential and enjoy the life God has handpicked for us.

Face your fear, achieve your dream

God encourages us that, "There is a time for everything, and a season for every activity under the heavens" (Ecclesiastes 3:1, NIV). If you are afraid of a new season approaching or uncertain about a decision that would change your life drastically, take a deep breath and be assured that it's going to end well. Whether it's your current opportunity or another down the road, God will give you the confidence to walk boldly into the next season. Talk with God about the decision you're facing, trust Him with the outcome, and don't let the fear of change hold you back from starting something that could be beautiful!

Fearless Girl

Use this outline as a guide to help you overcome your fear.

Recognize Your Insecurities: _____

_____

Face Your Fear: _____

_____

Identify The Lie: _____

_____

Discover The Truth: _____

_____

Find Freedom: _____

_____

Achieve Your Dream: _____

Fear of What Other People Think
(Ebie)

PRISON. That is where you'll be if you allow yourself to be enslaved to what other people think. I use the word "enslaved" because that is exactly what you become when you have this fear- a slave to other people's opinions. And listen to me loud and clear- YOU HAD A PURPOSE BEFORE ANYBODY HAD AN OPINION. We live in a society where every second of our lives is plastered on some social media platform and we base our worth on how many likes we receive. Do you realize how exhausting it is to live our lives in constant wonder of what people think of us? Girl, ain't NOBODY got time for that. We've got a lifetime of freedom and adventure waiting for us, unhindered by people's opinions!

Want to know the recipe for disaster? It's trying to be someone that we are not. Want to know the recipe for being fearless? It's walking in confidence and boldness in who God created us to be. Being authentic will always communicate what words cannot. And as far as I'm concerned, women who change the world are women who are completely themselves when they overcome their fear of others. Let us be women who sprint so passionately after the things of God that we don't have time to even consider the thoughts that others have toward us. Let us be women who never stop dancing with the truth that we were created for such a time as this! By being the woman God created you to be, you are inviting others to do the same. And that my friends is an anthem worth singing about!

Face your fear, achieve your dream

We overcome this fear by ingraining into our spirits what God says about us! You can be confident in the fact that Jesus went to the cross for YOU! This confidence allows us to live into our calling without fearing what other people think about us. We won't have to share every detail of our lives on social media because we will feel confident in ourselves and rely on the affirmation of God. Another important aspect of overcoming this fear is to transform the way you think about other people. Often, the way we think about others reflects something deep in our hearts that needs to be addressed. When we think about others through a lens of grace, we allow the same for ourselves.

Fearless Girl

Use this outline as a guide to help you overcome your fear.

Recognize Your Insecurities:_____

_____

Face Your Fear:_____

_____

Identify The Lie: _____

_____

Discover The Truth: _____

_____

Find Freedom: _____

_____

Achieve Your Dream: _____

Fear of Trying Something New
(Ebie)

I understand...trying something new can be terrifying. Going to a new school, going on a first date, or even going to a new coffee shop can stir up feelings of insecurity and anxiety. I remember having these feelings when Zac and I started our adoption journey. I came up with every reason why it wasn't the right time to move forward with adoption. After my spiel, I heard the Holy Spirit clearly saying, "Today is the perfect day to sprint after my heart. Take a step, and my faithfulness will do the rest." When you understand that the God of the universe is with you in everything, trying something new doesn't feel as scary anymore. So, Zac and I took a step of faith and watched God's sovereign hand do the rest. And it was in that season that we had our faith flipped upside down and turned inside out. We watched miracle after miracle unravel right before our eyes and now here we are, preparing to bring our two babies home.

Friend, you were made for big dreams that cannot be fulfilled inside the safety of a comfort zone. You see, there is this place called the ADVENTURE ZONE. It's in this zone where we ignore the nerves and bungee jump anyway! It's in this zone where we paddle out and give surfing a try. It's in this zone where we throw off the shackles of "what-ifs" and put on the robe of "let's do this."

Face your fear, achieve your dream

What would happen if we intentionally challenged ourselves to do something new everyday? I want to challenge you to write a list of all of the things that you have never done because you were fearful of trying something new. Then, try them one by one! Your list might include: get a bike, write a book, apply to grad school, learn the guitar, change the way you eat, go on a missions trip, find a reason to wear a fur jacket, forgive someone, go fishing, watch a new movie. Whatever the list consists of, just do it! And invite a friend to join you! Because inviting someone to come alongside you and join in fearlessness is always a good idea! AM I RIGHT? I imagine an army of women sprinting past the caution tape of comfort and relentlessly running after the dreams God has purposely and dangerously placed on their hearts. Try something new, and watch as your spirit becomes conditioned to choose the fearless thing!

Fearless Girl

Use this outline as a guide to help you overcome your fear.

Recognize Your Insecurities: _____

_____

Face Your Fear: _____

_____

Identify The Lie: _____

_____

Discover The Truth: _____

_____

Find Freedom: _____

_____

Achieve Your Dream: _____

Fear of Being Loved
(Esther)

A few years ago I had a huge crush on this gorgeous surfer. My friends thought he liked me, but I didn't believe it for a second. He seemed way out of my league. I didn't feel good enough for him at all, but to my surprise he asked me out! I wanted to climb on top of my roof and scream for the whole world to know how excited I was! When I went out with him, so many of my insecurities came to the surface. I overanalyzed everything about myself. I was so self-conscious and afraid that if he saw my true self he would lose interest in me. Instead of letting him come close to get to know me, I pushed him away. I had no confidence because I was so afraid of messing it up. My fear of being loved ended in sabotaging a potential relationship.

As crazy as it sounds, many people often live in fear of the very thing they want. Being loved can make you feel vulnerable and exposed. When someone loves you, they accept you fully, but do you believe that your unfiltered self is worth loving? Often, we answer "yes" to that question without truly believing it. If we dig deep, we might find that our sense of value has been marred by the faults we find in ourselves. We look at our stretch-marks, scars, thinning hair, crooked teeth, or awkward quirks and hide behind a filter of fake confidence. Sometimes, we may even get caught up in a fantasy about being loved, but in reality we are too afraid to actually believe it and let someone see past our filter.

Face your fear, achieve your dream

Do you get extremely physical in romantic relationships and use physical closeness to hide your true desire for being known and loved? Do you have a broken relationship with someone in your family and are afraid of letting them close? God says to you, "I have loved you, with an everlasting love. With unfailing love I have drawn you to myself." (Jeremiah 31:3, NLT) When you let God love you before all others it reveals your true worth. Choose one person in your life that you struggle with letting close and write them a letter completely unfiltered of how you feel. Include in the letter a solution to improve the relationship and ask them to forgive you for keeping them at a distance. Mail the letter or plan a time to meet with them in person. You are worth loving, believe it!

Fearless Girl

Use this outline as a guide to help you overcome your fear.

Recognize Your Insecurities: _____

_____

Face Your Fear: _____

_____

Identify The Lie: _____

_____

Discover The Truth: _____

_____

Find Freedom: _____

_____

Achieve Your Dream: _____

Fear of Not Having Enough
(Ebie)

Whether you were raised in a family that struggled financially, are currently 27 years old still eating cup of noodles, or keep thinking about that next big purchase, the fear of not having enough has a way of stifling our ability to be grateful. And when our gratitude is robbed, we become empty.

I've walked through seasons with Zac where we've wondered how we were going to pay the next batch of medical bills and still afford to eat. We've felt the stress and physical weight of this fear often. Each time it comes around, I become tense, impatient, unthankful, and I lose my perspective and trust. I've traveled to nearly 30 countries and have witnessed a lot of poverty. I've seen many people who do not have enough according to the world's standards. However, as other travelers can attest, many of the people with the least according to the world carry a joy that is unmatched. They're not paralyzed wondering why they do not have access to certain things. They are not crippled in doubt. They are not focused on what they do not have, but are simply grateful for the things that a majority of the world often takes for granted. I am sharing this point to acknowledge that it's heroic and noble to cultivate a lifestyle of thankfulness, for both the big and small things.

Face your fear, achieve your dream

We fall into the lie that God doesn't care about our finances, our health, and other needs, but that couldn't be more false! One of my favorite verses in the Bible is Matthew 6:26 which says, "Look at the birds. They don't plant or harvest or store food in barns, for your heavenly Father feeds them. And aren't you far more valuable to him than they are?" (NLT). There isn't one worry that has crossed our mind that God doesn't take notice of. Even more exciting than that, it is in these times of need that we realize that our vulnerable humanity has to be matched with the extravagant power of heaven and an increase of faith. When we stir up thankfulness, we recognize that God has the power over our circumstances. Whatever it is you're needing divine intervention on, thank Him in advance for His provision, promises, and perfect faithfulness! After all, a grateful heart is a breeding ground for miracles!

Fearless Girl

Use this outline as a guide to help you overcome your fear.

Recognize Your Insecurities: _____

_____

Face Your Fear: _____

_____

Identify The Lie: _____

_____

Discover The Truth: _____

_____

Find Freedom: _____

_____

Achieve Your Dream: _____

Fear of Failure
(Esther)

Bodybuilders use the phrase "lifting to failure" to describe the process of lifting until you can't lift anymore- where muscles have been pushed to their limit, causing them to tear and grow bigger. Despite the pain, failure has the potential to make you the strongest you have ever been.

It's a common belief to associate failure with a negative experience. Failing has the potential to make us feel embarrassed and ashamed and when we make a mistake, we automatically identify ourselves as being a failure. With this mindset, it's easy to believe our worth is connected to our aptitude to perform.

The fear of failure limits our ability to dare greatly and has caused many people to self-sabotage their dreams. If we allow failure to shame us, we lose confidence, stop trying and eventually give up. But failure is a natural component in the process of achieving our dreams. The truth is, failure gives us the opportunity to respond to life's challenges with a positive outlook and see beyond our present circumstances.

Failing doesn't define who you are, it refines you to become great. We must be vulnerable to the experience of failure and see it as a catalyst to fulfill our dreams. Recognizing our areas of weaknesses is actually an advantage because it helps us to discover what needs to be adjusted in order to reach our goal. With this perspective, our failures will begin to build our weaknesses and turn them into strengths.

Face your fear, achieve your dream

Don't be overcome by failure and live in fear. Instead, allow your failures to build your weaknesses. Letting go of past failures and confronting current ones will empower you to be stronger. Are you afraid of moving forward with an idea, dream, or conversation because you're afraid it won't go as planned? Write down the past failures that have held you back or the failures you are afraid of making and next to them write "I AM NOT A FAILURE" in big, bold letters. Know that God will guide you to make the best decisions even when you fail. God is with you, picking you up and showing you the way. Be courageous and develop a resilience for failure as you become strong in the pursuit of your dreams!

Fearless Girl

Use this outline as a guide to help you overcome your fear.

Recognize Your Insecurities: _____

_____

Face Your Fear: _____

_____

Identify The Lie: _____

_____

Discover The Truth: _____

_____

Find Freedom: _____

_____

Achieve Your Dream: _____

Fear of Socializing
(Ebie)

Oh boy, this is a big one for me! I once was surrounded by world-renowned speakers. While answering a question, I found myself frozen with the fear that I had nothing to offer these incredible people. I felt like my words weren't making sense and that I was not able to fully express what I was trying to! And I'm not talking about nerves here. I'm talking about that straight up fear that tells you to shut up instead of socializing. The devil came to steal, kill, and destroy. So you bet he is on a mission to steal your voice, kill your self-confidence, and destroy any relationships that could be built in response to stepping out.

This fear creates so many questions. Do they like what I have to say? Are they genuinely interested? Am I clearly communicating my heart? Let's turn our attention. Every single one of us is unique and valuable and we each have something to offer a conversation that no one else could! When we recognize this, our confidence increases and the fear of socializing diminishes!. Remember, words give life! And the words that you're withholding from the world in response to fear could change someone's world! So remove that inhibiting duct tape that fear put over your mouth and yell at the top of your lungs that what you bring to a conversation is valuable and important! Well maybe not literally, because the conversation may get awkward, but you know ;)

Face your fear, achieve your dream

I majored in psychology in college and thus tend to use the Myers-Briggs personality test as a compass for life. I am an ISFJ, so of course I used to mask this fear with the excuse that I was an introvert! But being fearless is NOT a personality type! As silly as it may feel, I want you to look at yourself in the mirror for a week straight and say, "What I have to say is valuable! My conversations today will encourage and edify someone! I will not withhold my words today!" Don't hold yourself to an unrealistic expectation that you won't ever say something ridiculous, because you will. And it will probably be to that Billabong model that you ran into, and that's okay! Let's stop taking everything so seriously and be women who can laugh when we say something silly, but still use our words to bring life to those around us!

Fearless Girl

Use this outline as a guide to help you overcome your fear.

Recognize Your Insecurities: _____

_____

Face Your Fear: _____

_____

Identify The Lie: _____

_____

Discover The Truth: _____

_____

Find Freedom: _____

_____

Achieve Your Dream: _____

Fear of Moving On
(Esther)

It can be intimidating to move on after a breakup, loss of friendship, or significant life change. We fear that what is ahead will be a disappointment compared to what we have left behind. We fear that if we hope again, we will get hurt again. Moving on to the uncertain future is difficult, but it is necessary to fulfill our dreams.

When I started surfing, I learned a valuable lesson about moving on. Waves would rapidly approach and as I would begin to paddle, I would continue to look back at the wave, afraid that it would crash on me. This resulted in me getting taken out by the wave and it happened over and over again. Frustrated, I talked to a friend about my experience, and she told me that I needed to look ahead in the direction I wanted to go in order to properly catch the wave.

I followed her instructions and immediately made improvements! Her guidance not only made me a better surfer, but provided a great illustration for life. If you constantly focus on what's behind you, it will distract you from the opportunity that is presently in front of you. God tells us to, "Forget the former things; do not dwell on the past. See, I am doing a new thing! Now it springs up; do you not perceive it?" (Isaiah 43:18-19 NIV). You are wasting energy worrying about the past, when God wants to do something brand new. You will never even be able to SEE what lies ahead in the future if you don't stop looking back.

Face your fear, achieve your dream

Letting go of the past is the first step to moving on. Is there a situation in your past that you haven't confronted? Addressing these issues is necessary in order to find freedom. Take time to journal about the memories that are holding you in a state of grief. Write down the areas that need to be addressed and the people connected to the situation. Pray that God would give you the courage to confront your past, forgive, and let go. Now it's time to start over. Recognize your habits that are hindering you from moving on and make small improvements each day. Look forward, anticipate a new and exciting adventure, and allow yourself to ride the wave of opportunity. It's time to turn the page and start writing a new chapter as you enter into the adventure of moving on!

Fearless Girl

Use this outline as a guide to help you overcome your fear.

Recognize Your Insecurities: _____

_____

Face Your Fear: _____

_____

Identify The Lie: _____

_____

Discover The Truth: _____

_____

Find Freedom: _____

_____

Achieve Your Dream: _____

_____

Fear of Being Stuck
(Ebie)

Whether in traffic or in a relationship, being stuck just sucks. I remember this fear coming to the surface when I first started dating Zac and was wondering whether or not our relationship was going in the direction of marriage. This fear is all too common, especially in the midst of big life changes. The devil tries to intimidate us by saying things like, "You'll be stuck in a boring marriage if you keep going forward. You'll be stuck in an unsatisfying job if you accept that position. You'll be stuck with no free time if you decide to have children. Don't do it!" We call it caution, but it is actually fear. Discernment and fear often appear very similar, however discernment is transparent and exposes something that isn't designed to be inside of you, where fear always wears a mask and prevents us from freedom.

I believe that the best way to overcome this fear is to embrace the season that you are in and sprint after what God has put in your heart. A woman who is full of passion knows that her Father in heaven has a purpose in everything. Even in waiting or seemingly stagnant seasons, God has weaved purpose and intention. God has an exciting, adventurous future for us and it might look completely different than we imagined. When we trust Jesus we are trusting that every season is an endless invitation to a wild adventure!

Face your fear, achieve your dream
Whenever this fear wiggles itself into my brain, I go back to a scripture from the Message version that says "What's next papa?" (Romans 8:15). Instead of fearing being stuck, let's try to understand how God is working! Let's embrace each season and weave passion into everything we do. Maybe you have a thousand passions? I do too! And that's what's so beautiful about the Kingdom of love- each passion is knitted into His eternal purpose and His heart. So write your passions down! Maybe it's helping end human trafficking. Maybe it's fashion, surfing, or baking! Whatever they are- write them down and put feet to those dreams. Intern at that nonprofit, go on a mission's trip, start a blog, buy a surfboard, invite a friend over to bake. I don't care what it is, just start living those dreams out with passion! Because the fear of being stuck will always evaporate in the presence of passion and freedom! Friend, you are on an adventure, so start living like it!

Fearless Girl

Use this outline as a guide to help you overcome your fear.

Recognize Your Insecurities: _____

_____

Face Your Fear: _____

_____

Identify The Lie: _____

_____

Discover The Truth: _____

_____

Find Freedom: _____

_____

Achieve Your Dream: _____

Fear of Dying
(Ebie)

June 11th, 2015. I'll never forget this date because it was the day my husband and I lost our first child at 9 weeks to an ectopic pregnancy (where the baby implants in your fallopian tube instead of your uterus). I'll spare you the long, intense details, but we were in Hawaii celebrating the life of my husband's uncle when the bleeding became so bad that we had to go to the ER. Upon arriving, the doctors kept changing the story of what was going on. It went from a blood clot, to a miscarriage, to having twins, to finally seeing the baby in a place it was not supposed to be. Because the baby was growing in my fallopian tube, it ruptured my tube, causing serious internal bleeding. I vividly remember the way the doctor told me that I needed to be rushed into emergency surgery within the hour or I could die. He said it so casually, as if he were the cashier at the grocery store, telling me my total for my groceries.

Whether you have had a near death experience or not, the fear of death can be crippling. When I experienced my ectopic pregnancy, I began confronting the truth that I would not be here forever and started creating a bucket list of things I still wanted to accomplish on earth. That's what we do when we have the fear of dying- we focus on what we are leaving behind and not where we are going. But let's shift our perspective for a second and recognize that we were created for heaven! When we have heaven to look forward to, we can live our lives with wonder and fearlessness!

Face your fear, achieve your dream
What have you missed out on because you were afraid of death? Don't give yourself the surface treatment here. Take a long, hard look and be honest with yourself. Was it surfing? Was it going on a missions trip? Conquering this fear is a lot like having a hard conversation with someone- all you want to do is avoid it. You imagine every outcome, it consumes your thoughts, and you know you won't breathe normal again until you just confront that person and talk through the issue. It's the same with overcoming the fear of death- you're simply having a much needed conversation with fear and addressing the beautiful truth that you've got too much life to live instead of being hindered by the fear of death.

Fearless Girl

Use this outline as a guide to help you overcome your fear.

Recognize Your Insecurities: _____

_____

Face Your Fear: _____

_____

Identify The Lie: _____

_____

Discover The Truth: _____

_____

Find Freedom: _____

_____

Achieve Your Dream: _____

Fear of Disappointment
(Esther)

Disappointment occurs when our expectations in life are unmet and we feel hopelessness. Even before disappointment occurs, however, fear can creep in and convince us that it is inevitable. The voice of fear invades our thoughts and robs us of the hope we once held onto. We haven't even had a chance to be disappointed when we prematurely decide that it will end that way.

I experienced the fear of disappointment when I applied to go back to school. It had been 5 years since I had any schooling and although I was excited, I was also really afraid that I would be disappointed. Thoughts plagued my mind for months leading up to school. 'What if I made the wrong decision? What if I'm meant to do something else?' Worry creeped in as I was consumed by doubt. I know I'm not the only one. This can be a common battle for many girls, especially when you are in the midst of a situation that is out of your control.

God gives us the key straight up in the Bible: "Having hope will give you courage" (Job 11:18, NLT). It doesn't say, "Lower your expectations and see how it turns out." Rather, it encourages us to get our hopes up! I found comfort and security in having hope and new thoughts began to come into my mind, 'What if this is EXACTLY what God has planned for you? What if you will be the happiest you ever have been? What if this is the next step to help you achieve your dreams?' Hope gives me the confidence to trust my decisions are good and that God will lead me. I don't have to hold back from fully expressing what I desire. Hope gives me courage to trust the process and believe for good endings.

Face your fear, achieve your dream

How can you have hope when you become weary in waiting? People will tell you not to get your hopes up, but I believe you should get your hopes up as high as they can go! Psalm 38:15 says, "Because I have placed my hope in you, LORD, you will answer." (ISV). When you put your hope in God, you can't be disappointed. The time of waiting is created for us to grow. What are you hoping for today that you are afraid will end in disappointment? What are the "what-ifs" that torment your thoughts? Write down the negative "what-ifs" and next to them write down the positive "what-ifs". Put your hope in God, and don't allow the fear of disappointment cause you to forfeit your dreams.

Fearless Girl

Use this outline as a guide to help you overcome your fear.

Recognize Your Insecurities: _____

_____

Face Your Fear: _____

_____

Identify The Lie: _____

_____

Discover The Truth: _____

_____

Find Freedom: _____

_____

Achieve Your Dream: _____

Fear of Abandonment
(Ebie)

Finding Nemo. We've mostly all seen it and if you haven't then cancel your Friday night plans and WATCH IT. I know it's a kid movie but I'm going to pretend you're like me and that every time it comes on you recite the entire film by heart. The movie is about a fish family and follows the journey of a dad who swims to the ends of the sea to find his son, Nemo. In the beginning of the movie, Nemo is snatched out of the ocean and dropped into a tank with multiple other fish that he has never met, forcing him into a situation full of the unknown. Nemo saw that he was alone and automatically assumed that he had been abandoned...a lie many of us believe all too often.

Maybe it was a break up. Maybe one of your parents left. Or maybe you are the only one in your group of friends that isn't married and having a van full of babies... You were once left feeling abandoned and alone and have no interest in revisiting that experience. The fear of abandonment often hinges on the feeling that God hasn't taken your dreams to heart and that He is M.I.A. Imagine that I am in front of you grabbing both sides of your head and yelling, "LIES, LIES, LIES. GIRL, get that outta your head!"

The fear of abandonment robs us of the truths that we are never alone and that He deeply cares about our hearts desires. Because in the same way that Nemo's dad went to the ends of the ocean to find Nemo, your Heavenly Father sent his son to earth to show you that his love will never abandon you. Friend, let's get this drilled into our spirits. God will never abandon you and NOTHING could separate you from the love of God (Romans 8:28).

Face your fear, achieve your dream
To break free from the fear of abandonment, I encourage you to dream! Dream like you've never dreamed before, and write those dreams down privately! Remember that the greatest adventure of this life will be to trust in the Lord and to run after the dreams He has put in your heart. The timing may not be ideal, and the route may even look different than you thought, but the end result will always be better than you could have ever imagined. Run fearlessly in your lane and watch His faithful promises unravel.

Fearless Girl

Use this outline as a guide to help you overcome your fear.

Recognize Your Insecurities: _____

_____

Face Your Fear: _____

_____

Identify The Lie: _____

_____

Discover The Truth: _____

_____

Find Freedom: _____

_____

Achieve Your Dream: _____

Fear of Commitment
(Esther)

Sierra and I had just begun our ascent on one of the hardest trails in Yosemite Valley: Half dome when halfway up the mountain I was ready to call it quits. It would take us 10 hours to complete the 17 mile trek and reach an elevation of 8,842 feet! The most hiking I had ever done was take a walk in a park. Let's just say, we were in for quite a rude awakening.

Thoughts of compromise ran through my head. I thought, 'This is good enough, let's head back. What's the point of getting to the top anyhow?' Relentlessly, my thoughts provoked me to give up. We continued up the trail singing songs and eating beef jerky to distract us from the pain. Although I wanted to give up, I was determined to finish what I had set out to do. And I'm so glad I did! The view from the top was breathtakingly beautiful!

I learned a valuable lesson on that hike to Half Dome: you have to be committed to the journey, not just the destination. The path you take to get to where you need to go might be boring at times, but it's essential to stay committed to the journey each step of the way. The fear of commitment is a common theme for many young people. The concept of signing a contract, getting married, getting a big girl job, or signing up for the fruit of the month club can make you feel, well...STUCK. Without realizing it, the fear of commitment can cause you to slip into an apathetic lifestyle as you opt out of plans with friends because you got a better offer or back out of a commitment because it was more work than you realized. Not all commitments are fun or easy. Some commitments are a process, but if we don't commit to the process we will never realize our full potential or achieve our dreams.

Face your fear, achieve your dream

When we fear commitment, we tend to run from the things that will challenge us to grow. Apathy causes you to settle for a temporarily fulfilling experience. There are sacrifices that come with commitments, but there is also great reward, and the rewards are lasting. Start making changes in your life by sticking to your word and following through. Make a commitment today to practice this new behavior and cultivate a heart of commitment. Decide today that you are going to be confident in your commitments and not settle for a life of apathy.

Fearless Girl

Use this outline as a guide to help you overcome your fear.

Recognize Your Insecurities: _____

_____

Face Your Fear: _____

_____

Identify The Lie: _____

_____

Discover The Truth: _____

_____

Find Freedom: _____

_____

Achieve Your Dream: _____

Fear of Not Falling in Love
(Esther)

As a little girl I dreamed of falling in love. I imagined it like something out of a Disney princess movie. Yet as I grew up, I was hit with the stark reality that it's not that simple.

Early on I became so afraid of never falling in love that I would have nightmares about it. It started when I was 7 and a boy liked me for the first time. He asked me to be his girlfriend and gave me a rose pin. I reluctantly accepted, red from embarrassment. Suddenly fear came over me and I thought that I was going to have to marry this boy whether I liked it or not. What was I going to do? My 7 year old brain was racing and it felt so real. I was betrothed!

As ridiculous as it sounds, fear has a way of escalating our emotions to believe worst case scenarios. For whatever reason, I believed that I would end up in an unpleasant marriage that was lacking in love. As I grew up, this fear continued to haunt me, making dating difficult and draining. I finally found freedom in my twenties when I began to confront my insecurities. I discovered that this fear had nothing to do with dating, but everything to do with me not seeing my true worth. As I worked through these issues, I was able to uncover the lies I was believing about myself and how I had idolized getting married, thinking that it could fix me. But falling in love romantically is not the ultimate dream. Life is full of opportunities to enjoy new experiences, and the adventure is found in waiting for each season to come in its perfect timing. You can learn to fall in love with so many other things like dancing, art, singing, or working out before you fall in love with a boy. More than anything, you need to learn to fall in love with Jesus. He is the ultimate dream.

Face your fear, achieve your dream
Do you struggle with seeing yourself as beautiful? Have you ever believed that you would have to settle in your marriage? If you answered "yes" to any of these, you are believing a lie. God sees you as worthy and beautiful, and He adores you from head to toe. To combat this fear write down 5 lies you have been believing about yourself, followed by 5 truths that God says about you found in the Bible. Whether you fall in love or not you can live in confidence that you are worth being loved not just by a guy, but by a world who is waiting for you to live out your dreams and purpose.

Fearless Girl

Use this outline as a guide to help you overcome your fear.

Recognize Your Insecurities:_____

_____

Face Your Fear:_____

_____

Identify The Lie: _____

_____

Discover The Truth: _____

_____

Find Freedom: _____

_____

Achieve Your Dream: _____

Fear of Feeling Emotion
(Ebie)

"If I cut off my feelings then I don't have to be vulnerable. Emotions are messy and for the weak. I don't have time." Yup, that is how I used to view feeling my emotions. I wanted NOTHING to do with them and feared that if I felt something, I would be told that I was wrong and my pride would be hurt. Then I got married, and realized I married a man that wanted to expose and address every emotion. We spent the first year of our marriage playing tug of war. He would talk through these emotions that I had been suppressing for 20 years and I would say, "NO, I DON'T WANT TO FEEL ANYTHING." But it wasn't until I exposed this fear of emotions that I experienced my greatest freedom to date.

Yes, feeling emotions can be scary, but holding them in and allowing fear to win is scarier. We were created with hearts that are meant to BURN with passion and compassion for this world! Emotions are a natural part of our existence and when we shut them off, we are shutting ourselves off from breakthrough also. This does not mean that we should welcome emotions that are out of control and irrational, but suppressing our emotions would be the complete opposite extreme. If I wouldn't have allowed myself to feel the emotions of sadness and anger about women trapped in the bondages of human trafficking, the Lord wouldn't have been able to use me to help fight it! Let's be women who are able to process our emotions through prayer and discernment and then allow God to use them!

Face your fear, achieve your dream

This fear won't go away overnight. It will take practice, practice, practice. Start by allowing yourself to recognize and process your own emotions. Sit in them for a while. Allow yourself to feel. It's easier for us to dismiss them, but freedom is found in facing your fears! Next, address those emotions through prayer. Talk to God about them. Then, use your discernment and the Holy Spirit to determine how to filter the feelings. Do you need to talk to someone else about them? Do you need to write it in a journal and move on? Do you need to write a song or a poem about them? Are they an indicator of something bigger that you are supposed to be a part of (ie fighting human trafficking or other injustices?). God will guide you when you allow Him to!

Fearless Girl

Use this outline as a guide to help you overcome your fear.

Recognize Your Insecurities: _____

_____

Face Your Fear: _____

_____

Identify The Lie: _____

_____

Discover The Truth: _____

_____

Find Freedom: _____

_____

Achieve Your Dream: _____

Fear of Losing a Loved One
(Esther)

When I was little I used to hold onto my mother and with tears streaming down my face I would ask her why she would have to die one day. It was a bit morbid for a little 5 year old kid, but what can I say, I have an old soul! I was so afraid that one day my mom would have to leave this earth and go to heaven. It was incomprehensible to my childlike mind and I was mad at God for wanting to take my mother away from me. Although I understand more now, I am still challenged by the fear of losing my parents or someone else I hold dear one day.

When someone passes away we feel a sense of loss, which creates the emotion of grief. Even imagining it creates a sensation of pain within our hearts. Grief is a condition of the heart that cannot be explained with articulate words or comforted by an affirmative touch. Only a love far greater than we could explain is able to exchange our pain with a peace that surpasses understanding. When you grieve something, you are learning how to let it go, putting your inquisitions aside, and allowing hope for the future to provide the closure needed in order to move on.

We can't keep people alive by worrying about them. So don't! God cares about our friends and family even more than we do and He wants you to enjoy your relationships. Rest assured that God promises to watch over you and your family. "So do not fear, for I am with you; do not be dismayed, for I am your God. I will strengthen you and help you; I will uphold you with my righteous right hand." (Isaiah 41:10 NIV) When we put our faith in Him to do what only He can do, we can have total peace and enjoy our relationships in the moment.

Face your fear, achieve your dream

Is your identity built around a certain relationship in your life? Are you holding onto people that you are afraid of losing- either having them walk out of your life or maybe having them pass away? It's time to face that fear and not let it rule you anymore. Set aside quality time to spend with your family and loved ones. Plan a family vacation. Call them regularly. Enjoy your relationships and make memories. Trust God to keep them safe, give you peace and be free from worry.

Fearless Girl

Use this outline as a guide to help you overcome your fear.

Recognize Your Insecurities: _____

_____

Face Your Fear: _____

_____

Identify The Lie: _____

_____

Discover The Truth: _____

_____

Find Freedom: _____

_____

Achieve Your Dream: _____

Fear of Settling Down
(Esther)

"I'm traveling to the Canary Islands for a surf trip for 3 months!" These were the words spoken to me from yet another friend who was trading in the American dream to live a vagabond life. I envied my friend and even tried to go on the trip with her, but the responsibilities of life kept me at bay.

My friend's decision was no surprise. Many millennials desire a life of gypsy living, backpacking, and wandering from place to place. The idea of settling down causes most young twenty-somethings to run for the hills. The thought of getting a real job, getting married, buying a house, and starting a family is scary! For some, these are dreams that energize their hard work. But for a lot of people, especially young adventure seekers, settling down feels like trading in freedom for a boring life.

It's common to feel bewildered at the thought of making such major life decisions, but the fear of settling down is an indicator of immaturity. Adventure has a place of purpose in our lives, but sometimes choosing to grow roots and build a sustainable life is the greatest adventure. The reality is this: fulfilling your dreams takes time, hard work, and commitment. Until we arise to the responsibilities that our aspirations require, our dreams will stay out of reach. Sometimes that means slowing down, focusing on what's most important, and prioritizing certain goals that align with our best future. Settling down doesn't mean you have to give up your sense of adventure, but rather is a shifted mindset that is focused on building legacy.

Face your fear, achieve your dream

Maybe the fear of settling down is causing you to run from the adventure you really crave: a stable future. It's time to take action and break-free from wrong mindsets that are attached to this childish behavior. Don't believe the lie that you aren't ready. You will never be more ready than this moment. It's time to change the way you approach your finances, relationships, and future goals. Let's get you started! Take some time to set financial goals and make a budget. Start saying no to short-term adventures so you can say yes to a lifestyle of adventure as you have more stability. Commit to an area of serving your church or community. Shake that fear of settling down by putting down some roots!

Fearless Girl

Use this outline as a guide to help you overcome your fear.

Recognize Your Insecurities: _____

_____

Face Your Fear: _____

_____

Identify The Lie: _____

_____

Discover The Truth: _____

_____

Find Freedom: _____

_____

Achieve Your Dream: _____

Fear of Going Unnoticed
(Ebie)

Do you ever feel like you're invisible? Or have you ever felt like you put in the hard work, only for it to go unnoticed? We have all been there, and my goodness it stings! I remember when I was first hardcore crushin' on Zac only to find out he didn't even know my name! I so badly wanted to stand out, yet as weeks went on, I somehow became even more invisible. It was emotionally draining! And all the girls that lost sleep on a crush said "AMEN." I experienced this fear when I first began working at Wipe Every Tear as well. I was planning my first mission's trip and wanted to be recognized for the amount of work I put into the setup...I'm talking colored tabs and customized travel itineraries! And when the trip came and nobody noticed the amount of work I put in, I was so discouraged! And if you pay close enough attention, you can count how many times I just used the word "I". When you're constantly in search of being noticed by other people, you become so turned in on yourself that you lose sight of the purpose behind the task and forget that your identity should be placed in the one who sees everything.

The fear of going unnoticed exists when we believe the lie that our value is found in the people that acknowledge us. My friend, listen to me loud and clear. A thought has never traveled through your head that was not noticed by your Father in Heaven. He sees you and He knows you. And maybe that is easier to read than to believe, but it is the truth. When He fashioned you before time, He said, "Wow. I've never seen anything like it before. The world was incomplete without her." Allow this truth to transform your mind and watch the fear of being unnoticed melt away.

Face your fear, achieve your dream
Complete tasks with the expectation that nobody will recognize what was done. Get dolled up without the expectation of receiving compliments. Have a heart that is rooted in the truth that God sees you and knows you. Open your heart to truly receive what God says about you! That is enough to sustain us. Now, share that truth with others! When our encouragement comes from God, we can freely and generously give it to others. Begin noticing what others are doing and don't be frugal with your encouragement...it will bless you as well!

Fearless Girl

Use this outline as a guide to help you overcome your fear.

Recognize Your Insecurities: _____

_____

Face Your Fear: _____

_____

Identify The Lie: _____

_____

Discover The Truth: _____

_____

Find Freedom: _____

_____

Achieve Your Dream: _____

Fear of Having Faith
(Esther)

I stood on the edge of a 30 foot cliff and looked down at the crashing waves below. It was a steep drop, yet all my friends were jumping off and having a blast! I took a deep breath. Did I have the courage to take the leap? There were no guarantees. A girl contemplated the jump beside me. She was shaking with fear, yet still desired to experience the joy of jumping. I knew my fear was irrational and that no matter how long I contemplated jumping, I would never formulate a reason that made it any easier to leave the safety of where I stood. I had to force myself to do it. So, I counted down from 10, closed my eyes, and screamed at the top of my lungs as I jumped!

The free fall felt like a sacrificial offering of my life! I was completely out of control. It was the most wild and freeing feeling as my body emerged into the ocean. I swam back up to the surface and let out a laugh at the invigorating feeling of total trust.

There is an aspect of having faith that can almost feel like a free fall- maybe even foolish and a little reckless. Before we step out in faith, our minds want to rationalize everything and run from the feeling of entering the unknown where we have nothing to cling to. But when we choose to step out in these moments, faith is in full effect. That is the space where we deepen our intimacy with God and our entire trajectory of life is transformed.

The best indicator that someone completely trusts in God is when they are willing to step into situations that require faith. I used to think I had a lot of faith because I grew up as a Christian. I thought it was the kind of thing that was hereditary and accrued over time, but I was wrong. True faith requires a personal decision and yields a personal experience. It wasn't until everything in my control failed that I had to take a leap and jump.

Faith begins when you get tired of chasing empty things and you find the things that leave you full. Things like talking to God and listening to him, reading the Bible (a book about God's crazy love for humanity), and doing what you love as you live with purpose. This is what having faith is all about- it's the greatest adventure!

Fearless Girl

Use this outline as a guide to help you overcome your fear.

Recognize Your Insecurities: _____

_____

Face Your Fear: _____

_____

Identify The Lie: _____

_____

Discover The Truth: _____

_____

Find Freedom: _____

_____

Achieve Your Dream: _____

Face your fears, achieve your dream

Something real happens when you take that leap of faith. The unexplainable assurance that you are never alone fills your heart and gives you hope. You were created to have faith in God and trust Him. The Bible says, "For in him all things were created: things in heaven and on earth, visible and invisible, whether thrones or powers or rulers or authorities; all things have been created through him and for him" (Colossians 1:16 NIV). Having faith changes our human experience as we learn to let go of our limited understanding and trust the one who created us. If you are afraid of having faith, get around some people who have taken a leap of faith themselves. What do you like about them? What makes them different? Why does their faith seem to affect them so positively? Don't be afraid of taking the leap to have faith and experience it for yourself. Having faith is the greatest adventure of your life!

FEARLESS FAITH

Now that you've completed the Fearless Girl book, we have one last secret to share on becoming fearless. Without this secret weapon, being fearless is powerless. That secret weapon is called having FAITH. Yes, without faith, fear will continue to have power over you.
In Romans 10: 10 (MSG) it says,

"It's the word of faith that welcomes God to go to work and set things right for us. This is the core of our preaching. Say the welcoming word to God—"Jesus is my Master"—embracing, body and soul, God's work of doing in us what he did in raising Jesus from the dead. That's it. You're not "doing" anything; you're simply calling out to God, trusting him to do it for you. That's salvation. With your whole being you embrace God setting things right, and then you say it, right out loud: "God has set everything right between him and me!"

Jesus died on the cross to save us from an empty and fearful life. Faith is our response to accept Jesus' invitation to a full and adventurous life. Faith means you put your trust in Jesus. No matter how hard we work, we will never be good enough in our own strength to find freedom from the shame that sin creates in our lives. Only Jesus can take that away completely and give us freedom and a fresh start.

If you want to experience this fearless faith, all you have to do is say yes to Jesus' invitation and start a relationship with Him. You can pray this simple prayer:

"God, I want to have fearless faith in you. I don't want fear to control my life any longer. Jesus, I ask you to take away my shame and give me a brand new start. I want to have a relationship with you and live an adventurous life with you. Teach me how to live fearlessly and love fearlessly. Thank you for answering my prayer, in Jesus' name, Amen."

Fearless Girl | Ebie Hepworth & Esther Marie

TRUTH BOMBS

Use these power packed truth bombs from God's word to combat every thought of worry and fear. Speak them out loud. Write them down on cards and put them around your house and watch as God's truth explodes into promises in your life.

Have I not commanded you? Be strong and courageous. Do not be afraid; do not be discouraged, for the Lord your God will be with you wherever you go
Joshua 1:9 (NIV).

Having hope will give you courage. You will be protected and will rest in safety
Job 11:18 (NLT).

Even though I walk through the darkest valley, I will fear no evil, for you are with me; your rod and your staff, they comfort me
Psalm 23:4 (NIV).

Fearless Girl | Ebie Hepworth & Esther Marie

The Lord is my light and my salvation— whom shall I fear? The LORD is the stronghold of my life— of whom shall I be afraid?
Psalm 27:1 (NIV).

I will instruct you and teach you in the way that you should go; I will counsel you with my loving eye on you.
Psalm 32:8 (NIV).

I sought the Lord, and he answered me; he delivered me from all my fears
Psalm 34:4 (NIV).

The Lord is near to the brokenhearted and saves the crushed in spirit
Psalm 34:18 (ESV).

Because I have my placed my hope in you, Lord, you will answer, Lord, my God.
Psalm 38:15 (ISV).

When I am afraid, I put my trust in you. In God, whose word I praise—in God I trust and am not afraid. What can mere mortals do to me?
Psalm 56:3-4 (NIV).

I'm proud to praise God, proud to praise God. Fearless now, I trust in God; what can mere mortals do to me?
Psalm 56:11 (MSG).

The Lord is with me; I will not be afraid. What can mere mortals do to me?
Psalm 118:6 (NIV).

Trust in the Lord with all your heart, and lean not on your own
understanding.
Proverbs 3:5 (ESV).

There is a time for everything, and a season for everything under the
heavens.
Ecclesiastes 3:1 (NIV).

So do not fear, for I am with you; do not be dismayed, for I am your God.
I will strengthen you and help you; I will uphold you with my righteous
right hand.
Isaiah 41:10 (NIV).

"Do not be afraid; you will not be put to shame. Do not fear disgrace; you
will not be humiliated. You will forget the shame of your youth and
remember no more the reproach of your widowhood
Isaiah 54:4 (NIV).

Long ago the Lord said to Israel, "I have loved you, my people, with an everlasting love. With an unfailing love I have drawn you to myself"
Jeremiah 31:3 (NLT).

Look at the birds. They don't plant or harvest or store food in barns, for your Heavenly father feeds them. And aren't you more valuable to him than they are?
Matthew 6:26 (NLT).

Therefore do not worry about tomorrow, for tomorrow will worry about itself. Each day has enough trouble of its own.
Matthew 6:34 (NIV)

Come to me, all who labor and are heavy laden, and I will give you rest.
Matthew 11:28 (ESV).

Peace I leave with you; my peace I give you. I do not give to you as the world gives. Do not let your hearts be troubled and do not be afraid
John 14:27 (NIV)

This resurrection life you received from God is not a timid, grave-tending life. It's adventurously expectant, greeting God with a childlike "What's next, Papa?"
Romans 8:15 (MSG).

And we know that for those who love God, all things work together for good, for those who are called according to his purpose.
Romans 8:28 (ESV).

For in him all things were created: all things in heaven and on earth, visible and invisible, whether thrones or powers or rulers or authorities; all things have been created through him and for him.
Colossians 1:16 (NIV).

For the Spirit God gave us does not make us timid, but gives us power,
love and self-discipline.
2 Timothy 1:7 (NIV).

Humble yourselves, therefore, under God's mighty hand, that he may lift
you up in due time. Cast all your anxiety on him because he cares for you
1 Peter 5:6-7 (NIV).

There is no fear in love. But perfect love drives out fear, because fear has
to do with punishment. The one who fears is not made perfect in love 1
John 4:18 (NIV).

About
Ebie & Esther

Ebie Hepworth

Ebie's passionate, relatable and faith-filled outlook on life has encouraged women all across the globe. Ebie is the U.S. Director for Wipe Every Tear and helps bring hope and healing to women rescued from the sex trade in Southeast Asia. Ebie and her husband Zac live in Boise, Idaho with their french bulldog, Atlas, and are in the process of adopting two sweet babies from West Africa.

Esther Marie

With an extensive background in youth outreach, mentorship, and anti-human trafficking initiatives, Esther founded Fearless Girl as a tool to inspire a life of adventure and purpose for young women. She is passionate about helping girls find freedom from fear to discover their true identity. A writer, surf instructor, and entrepreneur, Esther lives in Dana Point, California.

WHAT YOU GET:

6 VIDEO SESSIONS	4 EPIC DESTINATIONS	3 CRAZY CHALLENGES	ADVENTURE GUIDE
Experience wild adventure as you learn a step-by-step guide on how to face your fears and achieve your dreams.	Filmed in beautiful California, enjoy breathtaking views from Yosemite, Big Sur, Pismo Beach and Huntington Beach!	Test your courage as you are challenged to face your fears head on.	The Fearless Girl book guides you through the course as you become fearless.

WHAT OTHERS ARE SAYING:

"The Fearless Girl Adventure's course made me feel excited about going after my dreams. I never knew my fears were stopping me from being myself and achieving my dreams. I'm so glad I learned that in the course."
- Sara

"I always thought my life was boring and my dreams were out of reach. After watching the Fearless Girl Adventures Course I now know I have what it takes to achieve my dreams. I don't have to be afraid of having a boring life. I can have adventures too and use my dreams to help others."
-Andrea

 INDIVIDUAL PACKAGE:
COURSE & 1 BOOK $50

 GROUP PACKAGE:
COURSE & 5 BOOKS $75

 LARGE GROUP PACKAGE:
COURSE & 10 BOOKS $100

SAVE %15
USE CODE:
IMFEARLESS

Fearless Girl | Ebie Hepworth & Esther Marie

CONNECT WITH US

Have you been impacted by Fearless girl? Do you have a story about how you faced your fears and achieved your dreams? We want to hear from you!

 FACEBOOK.COM /FEARLESSGIRL.ORG

 @FEARLESSGIRLCO

 INFO@FEARLESSGIR.ORG

 WWW.FEARLESSGIRL.ORG

HELP <u>END</u> HUMAN TRAFFICKING

Do you have a passion to end human trafficking? We work in partnership with Wipe Every Tear, an international organization that is making a measurable difference in the lives of women rescued out of the slave trade in the Phillipines.

For more information on how you can volunteer, intern or go on a trip email partner@wipeeverytear.org.

ACHIEVE YOUR DREAMS

PEN AND PAPER NEVER FORGET

*USE THIS SPACE TO RECORD YOUR IDEAS, CREATE A STRATEGY,
AND HOLD YOURSELF ACCOUNTABLE TO ACHIEVING YOUR DREM.*

ACHIEVE YOUR
D R E A M S

PEN AND PAPER NEVER FORGET

*USE THIS SPACE TO RECORD YOUR IDEAS, CREATE A STRATEGY,
AND HOLD YOURSELF ACCOUNTABLE TO ACHIEVING YOUR DREM.*

ACHIEVE YOUR
D R E A M S

PEN AND PAPER NEVER FORGET

USE THIS SPACE TO RECORD YOUR IDEAS, CREATE A STRATEGY,
AND HOLD YOURSELF ACCOUNTABLE TO ACHIEVING YOUR DREM.

ACHIEVE YOUR
D R E A M S

PEN AND PAPER NEVER FORGET

USE THIS SPACE TO RECORD YOUR IDEAS, CREATE A STRATEGY,
AND HOLD YOURSELF ACCOUNTABLE TO ACHIEVING YOUR DREM.

ACHIEVE YOUR
D R E A M S

PEN AND PAPER NEVER FORGET

*USE THIS SPACE TO RECORD YOUR IDEAS, CREATE A STRATEGY,
AND HOLD YOURSELF ACCOUNTABLE TO ACHIEVING YOUR DREM.*

ACHIEVE YOUR
D R E A M S

PEN AND PAPER NEVER FORGET

*USE THIS SPACE TO RECORD YOUR IDEAS, CREATE A STRATEGY,
AND HOLD YOURSELF ACCOUNTABLE TO ACHIEVING YOUR DREM.*

54018672R00074

Made in the USA
San Bernardino, CA
05 October 2017